C000170816

CANCER

CANCER
June 22–July 22

NAME

SUN SIGN

MOON SIGN

RISING SIGN

Crystal Astrology for Modern Life

SANDY SITRON

CONTENTS

CRYSTALS, ASTROLOGY AND YOU

UNDERSTANDING CANCER

CANCER THROUGHOUT THE YEAR

LUNAR ENERGY AND MERCURY IN MOTION

CRYSTALS, ASTROLOGY AND YOU

THE STONES,
THE SIGNS AND YOU

The stars above you and the stones beneath your feet are part of the fabric of your world. Astrology offers a cosmic perspective. Crystals radiate with the healing energy of the Earth. Together, they serve as guides in your life, engaged in a vibrational conversation that can help you reflect on, and tune into, who you are. Birthstones and other crystals can be used to highlight and harness the energy of your astrological birth chart.

As above, so below – harness the power of crystals and the cosmos to create a deeper connection with yourself for a confident, empowered, high-vibe life.

Astrology is the ancient study of the changing positions and alternating energy of the celestial bodies and how this relates to our lives on Earth. The unique cosmic environment that you synced up with at the moment of your first breath provides awareness of – and offers a way to interpret – your personality traits, core strengths, growth areas, emotional style and so much more. When you better understand your vibrational self, it's easier to make informed choices about the big and small things in your life. Your conscious perspective is uplifted. Your mind is opened and activated.

Crystals, or 'stones', vibrate with the breath of the Earth. They act on an energetic level, sending vibrations out into the world. They are natural amplifiers of positive energy and bring discordant energies into balance. Each crystal has its own energy blueprint, which is why different types of stones may influence the human energy field in different ways. Pairing the insight that you gain from astrology with the healing power of crystals can help you navigate certain life areas and facilitate personal transformation and spiritual growth throughout the astrological year.

Crystals and the constellations call to us. In this book you'll receive a bespoke selection of crystals to help you amplify or balance the unique energies of your sign. You'll gain insight into your life, activate your highest potential and learn to live harmoniously with the energy that surrounds you.

When gazing at the night sky, when you hold a crystal in your hand, feel inspired to slow down, be present in the moment and get ready to embark on a meaningful journey of self-discovery.

YOUR UNIQUE RECOMMENDATIONS

We all accept that different things work for different people. Advice that's a perfect fit for one person might fall flat for someone else. Regardless of where Cancer sits in your personal astrology, this book will help you understand your Cancer nature and give you specific crystal recommendations for your sign and each astrological season. You can use these bespoke Cancer crystals to build confidence, spark creativity, feel more present, harmonize relationships, attract love, embrace your emotions, cultivate friendships, create abundance, optimize your health and wellness, and amplify your natural gifts.

YOUR ASTRO-CRYSTAL JOURNEY

Once you understand how the two energetic studies of crystals and astrology relate to your life, you'll be ready to take a deep dive into your Cancer energy and learn to use crystals to leverage the strengths of your Cancer gifts, whether Cancer is your Sun, Moon or Rising sign, or elsewhere in your unique astrology. You'll also discover your unique Cancer crystal recommendations for love, friendship, money, work and health to help you connect to your true potential and reach your dreams and goals.

As each astrological season holds a different kind of energy, this book will take you through the year and show you how crystals can help you channel your unique Cancer energy under each sign. In this way, you will learn to navigate through the seasons with ease and to harmonize with the cycles of nature. You will discover how crystals can help you embrace the ebb and flow of the 29-day Moon cycle, enable you to sail through Mercury Retrograde and even plan your week.

This book is part of a series that unites each of the twelve zodiac signs with recommended crystals. When you are ready to go deeper on your astro-crystal journey, you may choose to purchase the companion books in the series that correspond to the other prominent signs in your birth chart.

THE
STONES

Dazzling gemstones are typically formed deep under the Earth's surface, stimulated by the combination of mineral-rich water, heat and pressure. Subterranean 'gardens' nurture the formation of billions of atoms into highly ordered, three-dimensional repeating patterns to create unique crystals, each one holding a vibrational record of earthly, physical reality.

Across the world and over millennia, people have been fascinated by crystals. Lucent jewels have captured the imagination for over 30,000 years. In the Democratic Republic of the Congo, small tools decorated with Quartz have been found that date back to 33,000 BCE. The Ancient Sumerians of Mesopotamia (present-day Iraq) used crystals for rituals and magic in the fourth century BCE. Humankind has used crystals for decoration, status, currency, religion, healing, magic-making and, in more recent times, modern technology. Early radios used crystals as electrical and tuning components. Today's computers, LCD screens and some batteries rely on crystal technology.

Good Vibrations People across different cultures and generations have turned to crystals as guides or helpers because it seems that, whatever facet of earthly experience you are struggling with, there is a crystal frequency that can help you move forwards on your path. Crystals may help bring calm and heal stress, empower you when you need support or confidence, or provide focus and clarity when you're struggling with an important decision. Crystals are thought to absorb the energy that you are trying to release and release the energy you are trying to absorb.

For example, if you are feeling dull and listless, Carnelian may share with you a vibration of high energy and drive. If you are overheated or stressed, Rose Quartz may help you soften and relax. Choosing the right crystal that resonates with, or reacts to, your energy can shift your mood or your mindset.

CHOOSING YOUR CRYSTALS

In Part Two of this book, you will be guided to a selection of crystals that are energetically aligned with your unique astrology. If you are adding these stones to your collection, it's important to choose responsibly.

Sustainability and Ethics How did the crystal that you have in your hand make its way to you? The answer to this question is incredibly important to the well-being of humanity and the Earth.

The crystal industry is shrouded in mystery and plagued by bad practices. When you purchase a crystal, make sure to find gems that have a traceable, and short, journey from the mine to your hand. It's important to know if the mine that the crystal came from uses ethical, safe and sustainable practices. Discover if the lapidary, where the crystal was cut and polished, is a safe place that pays a living wage to the people who work there. The easiest way to do this is to mindfully source your crystals from sellers who have done the legwork. You vote with your financial choices. Make sure that you are contributing to better health and safety for all.

More information about sustainable and ethical practices and purveyors can be found on my website www.sandysitron.com/crystals.

Size, Finish and Price When harnessing the power of a crystal for personal use, the size of the stone doesn't matter. If you are holding a crystal or carrying it close to your body, its vibration is in your energy field and will have an effect whatever its size.

A raw stone is a stone that is untreated. These are just as effective to use in healing practices as a crystal that has been tumbled or polished. So when you are choosing a crystal, choose one that appeals to you, no matter the size or finish.

The stones selected in this book can be sourced at an affordable price. Although some of the stones mentioned may sound ultra-luxurious and expensive, these crystals are available at a range of values.

YOUR CRYSTAL
TOOLKIT

In the next section, you'll find crystal
recommendations for your specific sign. First,
here are a few indispensable crystals to round out your
toolkit. These selections are a wonderful support for
anyone at any time.

GROUNDING
AND PROTECTION

CLEANSING
YOUR ENERGY

Smoky Quartz   Getting grounded is the basis of spiritual work. So many factors in everyday life pull us out of ourselves. Spending too much time on your phone, not enough time in nature or eating too much sugar are common culprits, but the list goes on. If you want to nail your next meeting at work, remember where your keys are, or get on top of that to-do list, you need to get grounded. Feeling grounded also allows you to be present in your relationships and tuned in to your physical needs. This is where Smoky Quartz can help. This crystal keeps you centred, and emotionally clear. It may help you take a more practical view of a situation. On a more mystical level, Smoky Quartz has the effect of protecting you from energetic drains on your system. It is an excellent protection stone and just holding it can help you feel steady.

Selenite   Just as you bathe your body regularly, it makes sense to regularly cleanse your energy system too. Energetic cleansing can help you balance your emotions and clear your mind. Cleanse your energy after work, socializing or spending time in a crowd. Or employ Selenite to help you get rid of emotional residue after a tough conversation. Energy cleansing is also recommended when you are going through any kind of transition – a break-up, a move or some other important milestone. Use Selenite with the intention of purifying your energy field and cleansing yourself of anything that is dragging you down. Imagine that it shines a ray of light through your entire body, clearing and cleansing.

Smoky Quartz Ritual	Selenite Ritual
Perform the grounding practice on page 26 while holding Smoky Quartz to anchor you.	Selenite can also be used to cleanse the energy of your other stones. Place a Selenite stone next to your crystals overnight.

SOOTHING RELAXATION

Rose Quartz   We all know what it's like to get stressed out and frazzled. Sometimes the nervous system is overloaded and it's hard to calm down. When that happens, you need a soothing crystal ally that can help you relax. If you are having trouble sleeping, are feeling on edge, or are working through some challenging emotions, it's time to soften with Rose Quartz. This dreamy pink stone is known for its inherent ability to calm and reassure. It soothes you while strengthening your capacity for empathy and compassion. If you're feeling down, lonely or heartbroken, let this crystalline stress-reliever support you.

FINDING YOUR DIRECTION

Clear Quartz   Clear quartz is a true all-purpose stone. When you actively set an intention with Clear Quartz, the stone will magnify that intention. When your world is changing around you and you need to forge ahead in a new direction, Clear Quartz will get you there. Clear Quartz can help you clarify, strategize and set your aspirations for your life. Once programmed with your wishes and desires, this powerful amplifier will hold the vibration of your intentions and help you visualize and realize your future.

Rose Quartz Ritual	Clear Quartz Ritual
Infuse a tumbled Rose Quartz stone in your next cup of tea or glass of water for a mindful moment with a soothing elixir.	Write an affirmation that inspires you. Say your affirmation aloud while holding Clear Quartz.

INTUITION
AND INSIGHT

Amethyst Your intuition is your
natural guidance system. It's that gut
feeling you have when something feels
wrong, or when something feels just
right. Intuition shows up in different
ways for everyone but it's like a muscle
that can be strengthened. If you have
questions about your life and you want
to tune into the answers, Amethyst
is at your service. In those moments,
practice asking and listening and let
this violet stone help open up your
mind's eye. Amethyst is also a fantastic
friend when you need help saying
the right thing in your next important
conversation, meeting or presentation.
Or if you are looking for a sparkling
boost to your creativity, open the
channels of inspiration with Amethyst
by your side.

	Amethyst Ritual	

The next time you have a question about your life or
path, lie down and place an Amethyst stone on your forehead or
near the crown of your head. Meditate and make space for
the answer to come through.

THE SIGNS

ASTROLOGY AND YOU

You are a unique being, made up of a solar system of characteristics that define your identity. Astrology illuminates your personality and your path. It describes how you think, learn, love, act and much more. Astrology can also be used to understand the energy of the moment.

Astrology has been contributed to by cultures throughout the world over thousands of years. The astrology used in this book is drawn from contemporary Western astrology. Like all things in the universe, the movements of the planets through the zodiac create a vibration. At the moment of your first breath, this energy is mirrored within you.

Your astrology is much more complex than just your star sign. The movements of the planets under the zodiac, in the exact place, at the exact moment you were born form your birth chart, a personalized map of the sky from your unique vantage point on Earth when you took your first breath. As well as showing you where the Sun lands in your chart, denoting your star sign, it also shows under which signs the Moon and other planets fall – this is the key to understanding your personal energetic code.

In order to discover your unique astrological make-up first you need to map your birth chart.

SUN, MOON AND RISING SIGN

When someone asks, 'What's your sign?' they are actually referring to your Sun sign, but it's worth learning your Moon and Rising signs too. These three symbols are a good place to begin your astrological journey as they represent the basic outline of who you are – like a simple sketch that captures your likeness in just a few brushstrokes. Together these three symbols make up your inner and outer self.

Casting Your Birth Chart Go to www.sandysitron.com/crystals and enter your birth data in the 'Create Your Birth Chart' tool. You'll then receive your birth chart, also called your natal chart, that shows the signs that the planets were in when you were born, and where they were located in the sky.

SUN
SIGN

- The Sun is a constant bright light, it symbolizes your ego, the part of you that you consciously identify with. It's how you tend to think of yourself.

- The Sun is the gravitational centre of the solar system, it represents your core self and describes your fundamental character and values.

- The Sun is the energy source that creates life on our planet, it signifies how you channel your energy.

RISING
SIGN

- The Rising sign, also known as your Ascendant, is the constellation of the zodiac that was rising on the eastern horizon at the precise moment of your birth.

- The Rising sign shines new light into the world. It symbolizes how the rays of your personality beam out ahead as you walk down the street, meet new people, or interact on social media. It represents your vibe or your 'brand'. It epitomizes how other people see you.

- As you explore the following pages, you'll learn how to balance and enhance your unique energy using supportive crystals.

MOON
SIGN

- The Moon is most visible at night, it symbolizes the part of you that is hard to see – your subconscious self.

- The Moon changes shape through the lunar month. It represents your ever-changing emotions and how you respond subconsciously to your feelings.

- The Moon is a satellite that circles the Earth, it describes how you turn inwards to protect, nurture and soothe yourself.

PLANETS

SUN
⊙

MOON
☽

MERCURY
☿

VENUS
♀

MARS
♂

JUPITER
♃

SATURN
♄

URANUS
♅

NEPTUNE
♆

PLUTO
♇

DEC 22–JAN 19

JAN 20–FEB 18

FEB 19–MAR 20

MAR 21–APR 19

APR 20–MAY 20

MAY 21–JUN 21

CAPRICO

AQUARIUS

PISCES

ARIES

TAURUS

EMINI

AMETHYST

AQUAMARINE

JASPER

EMERALD

AGAT

DATES ARE APPROXIMATE AS THE DATES OF THE
SIGNS VARY BY ABOUT A DAY FROM YEAR TO YEAR.

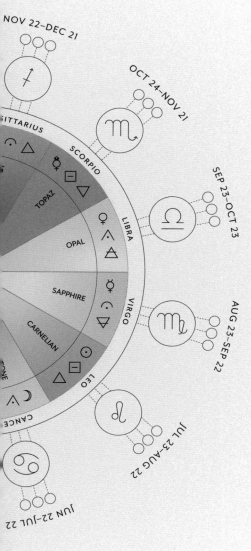

ELEMENTS

FIRE
△

EARTH
▽

AIR
△

WATER
▽

MODALITY

CARDINAL
∧

FIXED
☐

MUTABLE
⌒

NOV 22–DEC 21

OCT 24–NOV 21

SEP 23–OCT 23

AUG 23–SEP 22

JUL 23–AUG 22

JUN 22–JUL 22

SAGITTARIUS

SCORPIO

LIBRA

VIRGO

LEO

CANCER

TOPAZ

OPAL

SAPPHIRE

CARNELIAN

TOOLS FOR
YOUR JOURNEY

As you go forwards on your astro-crystal journey,
two key tools can help you gain insight and create positive
change – intuition and intention. Intuition helps you know
what you want and intention helps you make it happen.

LETTING YOUR
INTUITION GUIDE YOU

Everyone is intuitive, your intuition or 'inner knowing' is your built-in guidance system. Use the following prompts to strengthen your inner voice.

How to Connect with Your Intuition

Slow down Take a few deep breaths and close your eyes. The more you can slow down in your life (even for just five minutes) the louder your intuitive voice grows.

Pose a question What do you want to know? Ask yourself. Say it aloud or ponder it silently. Or choose to write it down, sketch it or even dance it out. However you pose the question, make sure it is clear. If you aren't sure what to ask, try, 'what do I need to know that I don't yet know?'

Listen for the answer You might hear words or notice a sensation in your body. You might write down your question in a notebook then flip the page and write down the answer. You might have an emotional response or feel compelled to move in a certain way. Pay attention.

Practice The more you practice asking and listening, the more you get to understand your unique intuitive voice. Just as weightlifting tones your physical body, practicing these steps improves your intuitive muscle, so stick with it!

21

INTENTION
SETTING

In your meditations and rituals, you can program
your crystals with the intentions or affirmations
that will help you meet your goals.

An intention is a new thought that you would
like to think. Our subconscious minds save
energy by putting certain thoughts and habits on
repeat. This survival skill has benefits, such as
giving us more energy and space for other things,
but it also has its downsides, such as getting us
stuck in a negative pattern. One way to break in
a new way of thinking is to intentionally repeat
a new thought. Here is how to 'affirm' your new
way of thinking into being!

HOW TO CRAFT
AN AFFIRMATION

Define what it is you would like to change.
Where are you feeling stuck? What is the pattern
that is bugging you? For example, 'I am stuck
because I have these exciting ideas for new
projects, but I never finish what I start.'

- Decide what you want
  For instance, 'It would be great if I
  finished my projects.'

- Make it an 'I' statement
  Such as, 'I finish my projects.'

- Make it affirmative
  Make sure your affirmation is
  positively stated. Say what you want,
  not what you don't want. So 'I finish
  my projects' not 'I no longer leave
  my projects unfinished'.

- Make it in the here and now
  Write your affirmation in the
  present tense: 'I finish my projects'
  rather than 'I will finish my
  projects'.

- Describe the feeling
  Include some positive descriptors,
  so that you can easily visualize
  how great it feels to realize your
  affirmation: 'I finish my projects
  and I feel so satisfied.'

- Evaluate Does the affirmation
  you wrote give you a positive
  feeling? If so, wonderful! You have
  your affirmation. If not, refine it.
  You may need a 'stepping stone'
  to make your affirmation more
  believable. For example, if you
  have a complicated track record
  with finishing what you begin, your
  subconscious mind may need more
  help believing 'I finish my projects
  and I feel so satisfied'. In that case
  try, 'I believe in the possibility
  that I finish my projects and feel
  satisfied', or 'I'm learning to finish
  my projects with satisfaction and
  ease'. With time and practice
  you'll find that you no longer need
  the stepping stone and you can
  update your affirmation to 'I easily
  finish my projects and I'm filled
  with satisfaction!'

WAYS TO
WORK WITH
CRYSTALS

Crystals are a powerful force as they are but,
in order to optimize their benefits, discover how
to care for and recharge them with regular
cleansing, and learn how to activate them using
the intentions you've developed.

CLEANSE YOUR CRYSTALS

Everything on Earth must go through a
process of decay and renewal. Cleansing your
crystals can help them reset with a clear energetic
frequency. When you cleanse a crystal, imagine
that you are clearing it of any energy that it may
have picked up from yourself, other people
and the environment.

How to Cleanse Your Crystals

Make sure to research your stone to discover if the method you are considering is safe for both you and the crystal. For example, some crystals may dissolve in water or fade in sunlight. Some stones contain trace minerals that may be physically harmful when released into water.

Light: Place your crystal in sunlight or moonlight for an hour.
Salt: Immerse your crystal in salt for about five minutes.
Sound: Chant or use an instrument such as singing bowls, chimes or tuning forks.
Water: Wash your crystal under running water, from a natural water source or a tap, for a few minutes.
Visualization: Imagine crystalline light or archangels surrounding your crystal with the intention of cleansing.
Selenite: Place selenite next to your crystal and leave in place overnight.
Earth: Bury your crystal underground for about a day.

When to cleanse your crystals

It's a good idea to cleanse your crystal when you first get it and about once a month after that. Cleanse more often if you use your crystals regularly.

GROUND
YOURSELF

Before you do any kind of energy work, it's important to get grounded. When a ship puts down its anchor in a quiet harbour, it's protected from being pulled by strong waves back into the sea. As you engage in energy work with crystals, you may drift and dream far afield. It protects you to have an anchor that keeps you connected to the Earth.

How to Get Grounded

- To begin, set yourself up in a quiet and comfortable space, either seated or lying down. Close your eyes. Imagine that your torso is like a tree trunk with roots growing down through your feet.

- Breathe comfortably and deeply as you imagine your roots flowing down through the ground and all the way to the Earth's core.

- Visualize a healing light moving up through your roots into your body. Imagine this healing light circulating through your body and carrying any tension or stress away and out, and back down into the Earth.

- Continue to imagine the energy flow – grounding energy coming up through your roots, tension and stress flowing back down to the Earth.

- When you feel relaxed and grounded, give thanks to the Earth before you open your eyes.

ACTIVATE YOUR CRYSTALS

Now that your crystal is cleansed and you are grounded, you can 'program' your crystal with the intention you've developed. Programming your crystal is one way to activate it so that its vibrations are attuned to your desires and goals. It's as simple as telling your crystal what you intend to create or achieve.

How to Program Your Intention

To amplify your crystal's power, focus your thoughts on your intention and train that energy towards your crystal.

- Make sure you have a clear intention or affirmation.

- Set a timer for ten minutes.

- Sit comfortably either in a chair or on the floor.

- Hold your crystal or place it on your body. You could also place it on the floor or on a table in front of you.

- On each inhale, repeat your intention out loud or in your mind.

- On each exhale bring your attention to your crystal.

- When you notice your attention wandering, bring your awareness back to the crystal and your breath.

- Repeat until your timer sounds.

CANCER

DATES: JUNE 22–JULY 22 ELEMENT: WATER
MODALITY: CARDINAL PLANET: MOON SYMBOL: CRAB
CRYSTAL: MOONSTONE

YOUR SIGN,
EXPLAINED

Nurturing, loving, gentle Cancer. You bring heart-centred compassion to the world. Cancer is the sign that opens the gateway to the world of emotions. Like a clear mountain spring or a desert oasis, your energy is refreshing. Others turn to you for nurture and support. You bubble over with love, especially when you remember to fill your own cup first.

The Cancer motto is 'I nurture', and you show your love through action. You dive in heart first, offering both presence and passion. You are passionate because you are deeply engaged with life. You just can't do it halfway – you are fully invested because other people matter to you as much as life itself.

Cancer is the symbol of the nurturing parent who creates the conditions for life to flourish and thrive. The Crab reacts emotionally but takes action when it's needed, to build supportive structures. Your Cancer energy shows when you start new projects, manage unexpected situations with care and compassion, spend time in your cosy home, and heal yourself and others. Your communication style is filled with unique expressions, sentimental ideas and passionate excitement. You love to recount old times.

Deeply sensitive, your feelings and intuition are a driving force in your life. As you give these intangible forces respect and priority, you gain energy and make better decisions.

CANCER IS A WATER SIGN

The Water element symbolizes the silent language of the spirit: it's the flow of emotions, the riptide of intuition and creativity – it's everything that you feel. Sensitive and deep, you have a strong connection with your inner emotional truth. You act with care and compassion and are focused on living a life that's true to your heart.

CANCER IS A PERSONAL SIGN

As the first of the three Water signs, Cancer is a Personal sign. Personal signs are playful and encourage you to explore without regard to outside factors such as other people, or the world around you. Before you reveal your emotions to others, your feelings demand a personal exploration.

CANCER IS A CARDINAL SIGN

The Cardinal signs correspond to the beginning of each new season. This energy helps Cancer initiate new projects and enjoy fresh beginnings. Cancer loves to take action and get things moving.

CANCER IS RULED BY THE MOON

Since your sign is ruled by the emotional and ever-changing Moon, you are highly sensitive to cycles of all kinds. Your mood is fluid, and you have the ability to go with the flow.

THE CRAB IS THE SYMBOL FOR CANCER

Like the Crab, you have a strong outer shell to protect your sensitive nature. The Crab moves between land and sea, symbolizing your ability to be both emotional and practical.

MOONSTONE IS A KEY CRYSTAL BIRTHSTONE FOR CANCER

Moonstone is a compelling crystal for Cancer. Choose it as your go-to support when you are sorting through your emotions, craving soothing and support, embarking on new creative projects, or desiring patience. This enchanting iridescent crystal helps you accept the challenges of the moment and tune into your emotions.

CANCER
TRAITS

Your key traits show how you shine.
These are the special characteristics
that make you unique.

Nurturing   You are a flurry of activity, busy doing the things you do for those you love.

Protective   It's not hard for you to stand up for others. You are loyal and caring to your core. You are also protective of yourself and your sensitive feelings.

Self-reliant   Wonderfully capable, you are good at taking care of yourself.

Intuitive   You are a sensitive water sign and, just like a crab sensing the tide coming in, you're ultra-aware of your energetic environment. This skill makes you psychic and empathetic. You lean on your gut instincts and trust your intuition.

Helping   It feels good when you can be there for others, helping them heal, and supporting them when they need a hand.

Perceptive   Because you're so emotionally tuned in, you generally know what's going on in your environment.

Cosy   You know how to make a cosy home and you love all things domestic. Your comfortable cove acts as a safe haven for yourself and others. You know how to make people feel warm and fuzzy.

Sincere   You are sincere and wholehearted. You can't do things halfway, so you go all-in. You act with honesty.

CANCER GIFTS
AND GROWTH AREAS

Your natural gifts offer both strengths and
challenges. The same traits that make you
special may also require balance at times.

Sensitive vs Moody   You are
sensitive by design, and sometimes
that responsiveness can morph
into moodiness.

Independent vs Dependent   You
can be quite strong and independent.
However, in a situation where you don't
have a position of authority, you may
feel dependent and act more childlike
than you really are.

Pep vs Pessimism   To be frank, you
can at times be pessimistic. But when
you develop your psychological strength
and emotional resilience, your naturally
peppy nature leads the charge. The goal
is to feel bigger than anything that can
happen to you.

Direct vs Indirect   Your feelings are
strong and can compel you to take
action. But if you become overwhelmed
by emotions, it becomes hard to make
the right decision or say exactly what
you feel.

Homely vs Hermit Crab   You are an
introvert, and you love to spend time in
your peaceful home. Strike the balance
carefully though, as too much time
spent at home can make you feel a bit
lonely and reclusive.

Reflection vs Rumination   You are
self-reflective, often gaining insight and
understanding about your true nature.
But if you overthink things, you may
end up in a cycle of rumination.

Compatibility is a complex feature of astrology
because you are more than just your Sun sign.
And other people are multi-faceted too.

Friends

Grounded **Taurus** friends steady your
ship. They are quietly supportive and
offer practical advice. You both love
comfort. On any given night you'll be
found lounging at home and catching up
on old times.

Virgo meets you halfway in your
goals of creating a productive and loving
world. Your time spent together is a
satisfying parade of to-do lists and errands.

Your **Scorpio** friends inspire you to
investigate the depth of your emotions
and they'll always be there with tissues
when you cry.

Pisces pals help you remember that
there is magic in the world. When the
two of you get together, time dissolves
and life feels more enchanted.

Foes

Gemini's attention is all over the
place. Your sensitive feelings would
be soothed if they would focus on you
more often.

Leo often forgets to mention
how grateful they are for your tender
loving care.

When **Sagittarius** gets on a roll
with their strong opinions and faraway
adventures, you'd rather feel safe and
protected at home.

Aquarius can turn your soothing
environment upside down with their
unpredictable ideas, schedules and
moods, leading you to crabwalk
sideways out the door.

TAURUS · SCORPIO · GEMINI · SAGITTARIUS

VIRGO · PISCES · LEO · AQUARIUS

CANCER
SUN

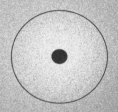

If you were born June 22–July 22, Cancer is your Sun sign
(check your birth chart for an exact calculation). Your Sun
sign describes your basic energy.

Just as the Sun is the centre of the solar system, your Sun
sign (also called your zodiac sign or star sign) symbolizes the
core of your being. As a Cancer Sun, you deeply value love,
family and trusting your gut instincts. You are motivated to
build a life that is meaningful and which includes the people
that you hold dear. Peace and comfort are your goals. You
devote a lot of your energy to others, especially those lucky
souls in your inner circle.

At times you need help pushing out of your comfort zone
and changing the status quo. You may benefit from spiritual
practices that help you work with your tender emotions.

Because your Sun sign fuels your confidence and
enlivens your sense of self, there are two recommended
crystals for Cancer Sun. The Amplifying crystal will help
you expand upon your gifts and the Balancing crystal will
help you integrate your growth areas.

CANCER SUN
AMPLIFYING CRYSTAL

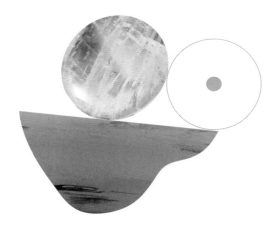

INTUITION,
WISDOM, SOOTHING

White Moonstone   Lean on luminous White Moonstone for its soothing and nurturing qualities. This pearly feldspar mineral can help you tune into your inner rhythm. There are times to expand and times to retreat. Let White Moonstone fill you with patience and help you trust in the moment you are in. You are creating your future slowly, and White Moonstone may help you feel safe in the present moment. The next phase of the cycle will reveal itself when the time is right.

This crystal ally calls you home to yourself. It invites you to lean towards your inner world. In this joyful dimension, time slows down and all is well. You can float, drift and dream.

Reach for White Moonstone when emotions have you in a spin and you need some comfort. When you seek profound insight, this glowing gem can help you access your inner wisdom. Anytime you need a little more patience in love or career let White Moonstone remind you how to flow with the cycles of your life. If you are being creative, it can help you with new ideas, projects and directions.

CANCER SUN
BALANCING CRYSTAL

CREATIVITY, VITALITY,
CONFIDENCE

Carnelian   When you are ruminating, feeling drained, or getting bogged down by confusing emotions, reach for orange–red Carnelian. This member of the Chalcedony family has a stimulating, fiery and warming quality. It offers vitality and courage that can help you push through and take action.

You have the ability to be quite direct, but sometimes you get caught up in emotion and waver, not knowing what to do. At these moments,

Carnelian may help you centre yourself and find your direction. Let the glowing sunshine of Carnelian warm your spirit so you can make moves and follow your heart.

Carnelian's activating energy may imbue you with confidence and pep so that you can do what you love to do – start new projects, nurture others with loving action, and feel pumped up with creativity.

CANCER MOON

PROTECTION, COMPASSION, NURTURE

In the same way that the Moon always appears to be changing shape in the sky, the Moon in your chart symbolizes the part of you that is always changing – your emotions.

Imagine that when you have an emotion come up, the Cancer part of you steps to centre stage. This happens throughout the day. It doesn't matter if the emotion is happiness, sadness, frustration or exhilaration – when emotions arise you go into full Cancer mode. Your loving, nurturing, sensitive and creative side is accentuated.

As the Moon is the natural ruler of Cancer, your Moon is very happy to be in the sign of Cancer. It's an astrological match! That means that you are always learning to be an emotional-intelligence expert. With practice and careful attention, you can sit with your feelings and listen to your heart. You prefer to be alone with your emotions until you can process them fully.

You are very tuned into cycles, especially the Moon cycle, so knowledge of the different cycles of your body and nature can help you understand your feelings. Your emotions are easily soothed by sharing them with people you love or being in places where you feel safe and protected. You are supported by a crystal that can soothe and comfort you while helping you tap into your compassionate and creative side.

Pink Mangano Calcite   Mangano Calcite is like a child's security blanket for Cancer Moon. This pink stone offers a soft cushion against the stress of the outside world. It comforts and protects. When you've had a long day, or your nerves are frazzled, keep Mangano Calcite close.

The energy of Pink Mangano Calcite is restorative. As it buffers and soothes you, you can return to your original state of love and compassion. This crystal's sweetness helps you connect to the frequency of divine love. And divine love has a tendency to overflow, boosting your self-esteem and helping you extend your kindness and nurturing to others.

CANCER RISING

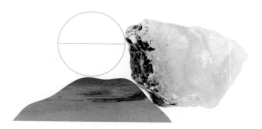

CONNECTION,
COMMUNICATION, CALMING

Your Rising sign is the sign that was on the eastern horizon when you were born, it represents the face you show to the world – your social personality. As a Cancer Rising, you shimmer with a loving energy that reassures others and puts them at ease. When you enter a room, your vibe is soothing, affectionate and a bit self-protective. If you're invited into a group of new people, you'll take a minute to warm up to them. However, your energy is like a beacon that others gravitate to for comfort. More than one stranger has cried on your shoulder. Once someone has been lucky enough to make it into your inner circle, they are a friend for life.

When it comes to group endeavours, you're a competent leader but you may prefer to help from behind the scenes. You have big ideas, and your compassionate nature wins approval from others. When you're in a good mood, everyone feels warmed by your care and attention.

As a Cancer Rising, you are aided by a crystal that offers you objectivity and optimism so that you can reflect bright light out into the world – and maybe even shine a little moonlight on yourself while you're at it.

Blue Chalcedony   As a Cancer Rising, you yearn to connect with others, but sometimes emotions stand in your way. Let soft and translucent Blue Chalcedony help you think clearly and objectively so that you can communicate with ease.

If you've been swimming in deep emotional waters, Blue Chalcedony can help you come up for a breath of fresh air. This crystal has a way of offering a new perspective, maybe even bestowing a dose of optimism. With a more light-hearted outlook, you may feel inclined to be less self-critical. Choose this crystal when you want to look on the bright side or treat yourself and others with kindness.

OTHER CANCER SUPPORT CRYSTALS

The following crystals are helpful for all Cancer placements – your Sun, Moon, Rising Sign and any other Cancer planet or point you may have in your chart. Harness the potential of these stones for clarity and ease in important life areas.

Everyone has different goals for romantic love. And your wishes or desires can change over time. You may wish to attract or pursue love. Or maybe you are hoping to deepen your ability to love, or open up to intimacy physically, emotionally or spiritually. As a Cancer, you are nurturing and devoted in loving relationships. Quality time spent together is important to you. You are often doing caring things for your object of affection, even if these acts of service sometimes go unnoticed. Memories and mementos are treasured – you have overflowing boxes of ticket stubs and love letters that remind you of special moments. You need a crystal that helps you relax and receive love, while soothing your emotions.

RELAXATION
PEACE
PROTECTION

Pink Opal Cancer, love is your specialty. You usually show your love by taking care of others. When you want love to take on a different energy, reach for Pink Opal. With this gem by your side, you become filled with peace and tranquility. Instead of relying on how much you can do for your lover, you can enjoy just being with them. With its playful and relaxing vibes, Pink Opal may help you attract new love. Or, if you're in an existing partnership, Pink Opal may help you chill out so that you can feel present and supported. By soothing any anxiety or fear, this divine crystal protects your tender heart. This is important because you are naturally so open-hearted and loving, you sometimes need a small buffer so that you feel safe to take risks in relationships.

CANCER X FRIENDSHIP

Friends offer support, fun, love and new perspectives. With Cancer prominently placed in your chart you are a sincere and affectionate friend. You cherish your alone time, but you also love to be surrounded by your trusted inner circle. You support your friends in a way that makes them feel protected and cared for, although sometimes you have a hard time letting them do their own thing. In friendship, you are well served by a crystal that helps you feel energized and vitalized so you can do what you love to do – be a caring and involved friend!

Ruby Fuchsite You're the friend who organizes the get-togethers. When a buddy is sick, you're first on the scene with homemade soup and a good movie. Your thoughtfulness knows no bounds and demands a lot of energy. When you need to refill your cup, reach for Ruby Fuchsite. This pale green and magenta crystal boosts your life force and helps you make excellent choices. It has a way of helping you feel strong and independent, so that you easily know how to balance your own needs with the needs of other people. With this vitalizing Ruby Fuchsite by your side, you're energized and ready to get involved. When you need a little time alone, this dazzling crystal can help you nurture yourself, too.

REVITALIZATION

ENERGY

NURTURE

Astrological insight can help increase your money-making potential. Your Cancer prosperity gifts are empathy, management skills, honesty, devotion, hospitality, family, intuition and healing, so look to these qualities for inspiration. How might your family support you or inspire you in meeting your financial goals? How could listening to your intuition help you when it comes to money and finances? As a Cancer, your money-management habits need to feel directly connected to your goals for your home, family and philanthropy. You love to start new projects and make plans. Get your family (or your chosen family) involved in your financial goals. Focus on pursuits that feel heart-driven. Emotions can propel your spending habits, so make sure you have a solid plan to follow.

**BLISS
COURAGE
RADIANCE**

Ruby If you are ever feeling uncertain, let Ruby bring you a dose of bliss, possibility and passion. This sweetly cheerful scarlet gem can give you the gumption that you need to take on the world. You already have excellent interpersonal skills that help you make money. But when you crave more drive and courage, reach for Ruby to give you a boost. It may prompt you to take the lead or step out of your comfort zone.

CANCER × WORK

Your ideal career finds you taking the lead on projects that are close to your heart and core values. Even though you tend towards the comfort of familiarity, you thrive when you take risks at work. When you feel at home with the people you work with, your productivity levels soar. Trying to keep your heart and emotions out of your work will stifle you; instead, you need to find a work environment where you can be your creative, spontaneous, emotional and sometimes messy best self. You need to learn to set healthy boundaries, trust your gut instinct, and work with the ebb and flow of your natural energy cycles. For work support, look for a crystal that helps you connect with your intuition so that you can trust your decisions and build confidence in yourself.

Moonstone Tourmaline   Some people look for crystals to inspire them to be fearless and action-oriented at work, but you are best served by a crystal that connects you with your intuition, so that you feel aligned with your professional decisions on all levels of heart and mind. And you can always use an extra dose of logic to help you make practical choices with your time and money. So, reach for Moonstone Tourmaline to help you on your career journey. This sparkling white and speckled black stone comprises both White Moonstone and Black Tourmaline. It delivers a blend of intuition and logic that can help you trust yourself, make solid plans and know when it's time to rest and time to push forwards.

INTUITION
LOGIC
SELF-TRUST

As a fluid Water sign, your health and energy levels are highly cyclical. Your circadian rhythm, the lunar cycle, a menstrual cycle (if you have one), and the cycle of the seasons are all unseen forces that you may be responding to at any given moment. Awareness of these cycles will help you make sense of your energy levels and plan your life. Constancy in the things that you can control, such as diet and exercise, can help you feel grounded. Your emotions and health are deeply connected, so honouring your emotions every day and working with a trusted therapist or counsellor will have a wonderful effect on your physical health. You need a crystal that will help you honour your emotions and let you feel energized and grounded.

RELEASING
PATIENCE
ACCEPTANCE

Black Moonstone Black Moonstone helps you stay quietly with whatever is happening in your body, mind and spirit. This gun-metal grey and brown crystal helps you recognize your emotions, accept the cycles and let old patterns dissolve. It bestows upon you the strength of patience. When you deny how you're feeling, you end up feeling disconnected. Black Moonstone lets you return home to yourself and feel rooted, while helping you to honour your emotions. Together, this supports your overall well-being. To accept things that are changing in your life, or to protect your emotional self, reach for Black Moonstone.

CANCER
THROUGHOUT
THE YEAR

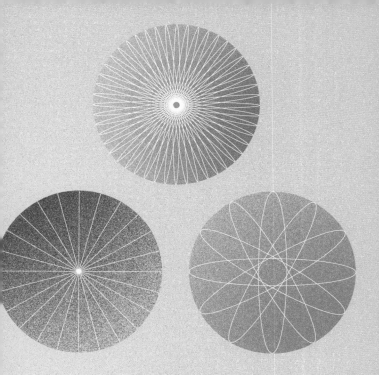

The energies of the zodiac signs affect us throughout the
ear. In astrology, there is a season for everything. Feeling
eparated from nature's cycles and rhythms can make you
eel out of step or off-kilter. It may add to stress and drain
nergy. Understanding and attuning to astrology's seasons
night help you feel enlivened.

Take this attunement one step further by using crystals to
mplify the unique energy of each moment, so that you feel
lly aligned with the rhythms of nature.

The following pages take you on a journey with the sun
s it passes through the twelve signs of the zodiac on its
nnual rotation. You will discover the key energies of each
eason, along with a sign-specific horoscope that aligns with
e important themes of your unique chart.

CONFIDENCE AND LEADERSHIP

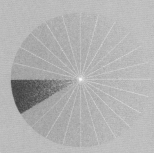

Aries season is the signal that begins the horse race. And they're off! This is the moment to gallop at top speed towards your goals. Put yourself out there with confidence. Make bold decisions and step in time with your intuition. This season is about saying YES to who you are and living your life with freedom. The buds are beginning to emerge and new life is beginning. Sync up with this feeling of potential and possibility.

CANCER HOROSCOPE FOR ARIES SEASON

The energy and vitality of this season can be funnelled into your work. The Sun is touring the area of your chart that rules ambition, career and public influence. Find some time to strategize and re-evaluate. Whether your plans revolve around a project or a goal, you want your efforts to feel as if they are adding up to something concrete.

Affirmation

I AM ENOUGH AND I AM READY.

Morning Practice

Get your heart rate up with
some fiery cardio exercise.

Evening Practice

Cool down that inner
fire with a soothing herbal tea.

CRYSTALS FOR
ARIES SEASON

CONFIDENCE

Hessonite Garnet   Developing confidence is a practice of
establishing deep self-trust. Let Hessonite Garnet's activating
and powerful energy help you build up your courage so that
you can just go for it. Also try Green Aventurine, Orange
Calcite or Malachite.

LIVING BOLDLY

Pink Aventurine   When the time is ripe for taking bold
action, Pink Aventurine can help you advance into your next
adventure. Reach for it when you need a boost of fun. This
spirited crystal connects you with your heart centre, and acts
as your best accomplice in bravery and boldness. Or choose
Ruby, Tangerine Quartz or Sardonyx.

DRIVE

Fire Agate   Aries season is the vehicle in which to follow
your passions and desires, which makes Fire Agate the
gasoline. Whether you need to get an important project
going or just tackle spring cleaning, put yourself on track to
get things done by syncing up with the vibration of this fierce
crystal. You could also reach for Bloodstone, Stromatolite or
Cinabrite.

MONEY AND
SELF-WORTH

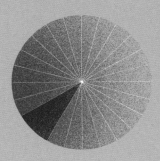

Like working in a garden and then enjoying the beauty that
you've cultivated, Taurus represents sustained effort that
leads to a productive reward. This season is the prime time
to focus on building up your sense of personal worth and
value. On one level, this process may involve nurturing your
self-esteem. On another level, this may include thinking
about security, money and finances. Taurus season is also a
time to remember the beauty of life. It reminds us that no
matter what is going on, there are simple pleasures to be had

CANCER HOROSCOPE
FOR TAURUS SEASON

This is your moment to dream. With
the Sun lighting up your zone of
community and the future, you may feel
inspired to think bigger and connect
with a vast social network. In practical
terms, this could be as simple as
cultivating a new friendship or crafting
a fresh vision board to get your dreams
and hopes down on paper. Make new
mental and social connections.

Morning Practice

Practice gratitude by reminding
yourself of three things you're
grateful for.

Evening Practice

Do something that feels good to
your body, like stretching or
wearing soft clothing.

CRYSTALS FOR
TAURUS SEASON

MONEY MAGIC

Green Jade   No matter where you are beginning
financially, Green Jade will juice up your money situation.
This abundance stone has a way of amplifying your potential.
A soft and expansive prosperity stone that soothes the spirit, it
will support you as you make wise financial decisions. Reach
for it when you crave a feeling of security. You could also use
Pyrite, Emerald or Epidote.

SELF-WORTH

Red Jasper   Red Jasper will amp up your self-appreciation
quotient. Choose Red Jasper when you're feeling uncertain,
if your confidence could use a boost, or if you want to
feel more resilient in any way. This stone will get you in
the groove of trusting your own value. Also try Carnelian,
Chrysocolla or Bixbite.

ABUNDANCE

Green Apatite   If you are feeling like something in your life
is lacking, such as money, time, energy, sleep, or support, for
example, you might need to boost your sense of abundance.
Taurus season is the perfect time to grasp hold of that feeling
of nature's plentifulness. Use Green Apatite to replenish your
energy and help you feel satisfied and satiated with what you
have. You could also reach for Golden Tourmaline, Uvarovite
Garnet or Agate.

VALUES
AND COMMUNITY

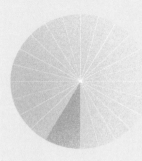

Gemini energy is like a buzzing bee that moves from
flower to flower in a garden. This season is a time of mental
stimulation, new ideas, learning, communicating and
sharing. Use Gemini season to evaluate or challenge your
mindset and values. Which attitudes are no longer serving
you? What's truly important to you? Gemini season is also
a time to connect with others in the community. What can
you learn from others? What can you teach others? It's a fun
and lively season full of new connections.

CANCER HOROSCOPE
FOR GEMINI SEASON

How do you relax and slow down? The
Sun is pointing your attention towards
introspective themes – emotions,
spirituality, inner truth, dreams and
intuition. Even though Gemini season
is generally a social time, the influence
of the Sun in your chart invites you to
retreat. Make sure you have enough
time to meditate and dream.

Morning Practice

Help a new mindset emerge with a potent Gemini season intention.

Evening Practice

Before falling asleep, envision yourself having a great time at a party surrounded by everyone you love.

CRYSTALS FOR
GEMINI SEASON

MASTER YOUR MINDSET

Heliodor   Have repeating thoughts, fears or anxieties been plaguing you? Use the revitalizing energy of Gemini season and Heliodor to hit the reset button on these old thought patterns. This stone will gently help you harmonize your thoughts and adjust your mindset, helping you reconnect with your true values. Alternatively, try Blue Lace Agate, Chrome Chalcedony or Dragonstone.

CONNECTING

Agatized Coral   When you really want to feel connected, seen, heard and understood, reach for Agatized Coral. This fossilized coral nudges you to reach out to others and helps you analyse your relationships, whether with friends, lovers, family, neighbours or colleagues. It relays an upbeat feeling so that you can view your relationships with the people in your life with optimism. You may also choose Citrine, Apricot Agate or Bismuth.

COMMUNICATION

Aquamarine   Aquamarine is your crystal-clear communication companion. Communication helps us feel connected, and allows us to learn and grow. In those moments when you feel confused or foggy, this elegant stone will help you become grounded and steady. Use Aquamarine to find your voice – it will help you tune into your own true message and the truth of those around you. Alternatively, reach for Turquoise, Prairie Tanzanite or Green Chrysocolla.

HOME AND NURTURE

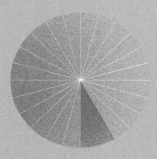

Come on home to Cancer season. Like Cancer's symbol, the Crab, wrap yourself in a protective shell and reflect on your life and your feelings. In Cancer season, engage in meaningful self-care, and also put your energy into nurturing others. Discover what makes you feel safe and cosy. This could be your actual home, your closest relationships or tending to the feelings and needs of your inner child.

CANCER HOROSCOPE FOR CANCER SEASON

Prepare to surprise yourself! You have so much to share with the world. And you might just feel ready to put it all out there. The Sun is illuminating your zone of identity and personality.

That means it's time to be yourself! Do the things that make you feel like you. Be brave and courageous, but most of all, have fun.

<table>
<tr><td>Morning Practice</td><td>Evening Practice</td></tr>
<tr><td>Let your inner child take the lead: what do they want to do today?</td><td>Sing a lullaby to soothe your inner child before bed.</td></tr>
</table>

NURTURING

Blue Calcite What do you want to actively care for? Yourself? A child? A creative project? In order to feel truly nurturing, you need to feel inspired by love. Blue Calcite will help you soften and open up your heart centre, so that you feel drawn to put your compassionate and attentive energy where it is needed most. Other nurturing crystals include Moonstone, Blue Chalcedony and Bumblebee Jasper.

HOME ENVIRONMENT

Pink Mangano Calcite Home is where you are safe and protected. It's your emotional nest where you can relax. Use Pink Mangano Calcite to create a grounded and peaceful home environment. This stone acts as a balm that will help you feel harmonized. Place this rosy crystal in your inner sanctum and set the intention to soothe conflict and soften your environment so that you can restore your energy after a long day or week. You could also try Chiastolite, Rose Quartz or Peach Moonstone.

FAMILY BONDS

Bornite Family, whether chosen or blood-related, represent some of our closest relationships. Use Bornite to foster the strength of family relationships. This is a joyful stone that will help you embrace the positives that come from your family circle, while at the same time grounding you to help you remember who you are as an individual. Also try Orange Calcite, Indigo Gabbro or Girasol Quartz.

CREATIVITY
AND FUN

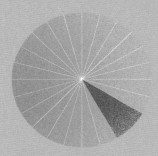

Harnessing your creativity and expressing your true self with others, that's the key to making the most of Leo season. It's all about playful sharing and creative shining. Radiate your magnificent heart of gold outwards with immediacy, freedom, spontaneity, generosity and a giant sense of fun. During this season of wholehearted self-expression, take a little time to remember how unique you are. Remember what inspires you and reflect on what you love most about yourself.

CANCER HOROSCOPE
FOR LEO SEASON

Turn your attention to practical matters. The Sun is lighting up your zone of money and worth, so it makes sense to do a financial review. Make sure your values are reflected in your budget. In addition, it's an excellent time to build up your self-worth and confidence – doing this will help you feel strong and resilient.

Morning Practice

Create daily.

Evening Practice

Seek out a chance to laugh every day and go to bed with a smile on your face.

CRYSTALS FOR
LEO SEASON

INSPIRATION

Rutilated Quartz   Inspiration is the creative spark and Rutilated Quartz can help you turn that spark into a roaring bonfire. Make Leo season feel lit up with creativity. Keep Rutilated Quartz by your side when you need an inventive solution to a problem at work, when your love life could use an inspiring reboot, or when you are ready to awaken the artist within. Set your intentions and let this highly programmable stone carry the flame of your dreams. You could also use Sunstone, Golden Labradorite or Yellow Sapphire.

SELF-APPRECIATION

Thulite   Leo season is the time to shed all insecurities and put your faith in your one true self. Loving yourself dissolves insecurity and self-criticism. Thulite tunes you into the vibration of love, peace and harmony, allowing you to be present and wholly yourself. Alternatively, reach for Ruby, Larimar, or Desert Jasper.

COURAGE

Golden Apatite   To ensure your lion-heartedness knows no bounds, you need to fire up your courage. Golden Apatite bestows upon you both passion and discernment, which determine which fears are baseless. Use it when you need to take a risk at work, strike up a conversation with someone you admire or stand up for your values. Other courage-giving crystals are Carnelian, Iolite-Sunstone or Citrine.

59

HEALTH
AND HABITS

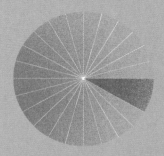

Our goals and dreams require a big-picture view,
but Virgo season reminds us that life is actually lived in the
small details. Focus on how you are living your life, your
everyday routines and rituals. On a practical level, what is
important to you? Virgo energy helps you take a closer
look at your health and habits, and how you can be
of service to others as well.

CANCER HOROSCOPE
FOR VIRGO SEASON

Illuminate your mind by getting
curious. Ask the questions that inspire
you and define a field of study that
excites you. The Sun is in your sector of
learning and communication so it's an
excellent time to write, teach or learn.
Your local community can also give
you a deep feeling of belonging. Enjoy
connecting and sharing.

Morning Practice

Drink a glass of water
first thing.

Evening Practice

Write down one task you're
going to complete tomorrow,
and stick to it.

CRYSTALS FOR
VIRGO SEASON

FOCUS

Clear Quartz   Virgo season ushers in a chance to notice the
details and get focused. Use Clear Quartz to take you all the
way there. This cleansing stone helps you rivet your attention on
your commitments. When you program Clear Quartz with your
intention for focus, you'll find that it supports you, whether you
have a tight deadline or you just really need to concentrate. You
could also turn to Vanadinite, Amazonite or Tiger Iron.

HEALTH

Chevron Amethyst   A lot of factors go into maintaining
optimum health: genetics, diet, exercise, access to care, to
name just a few. Virgo season energy will encourage you
to think wisely about the preventative measures that you
can take to boost both your mental well-being and physical
health. Use Chevron Amethyst for gentle motivation that can
help you happily embrace healthier choices. Or try Girasol
Quartz, Ruby Fuchsite or Black Tourmaline.

ALTRUISM

Stromatolite   Humanity wouldn't be a successful species
without the desire to be of service to others. Virgo season plus
Stromatolite is your recommendation for kindness and selfless
action. Turn your attention to what you can do to help others,
whether that's volunteering, making a donation to a good
cause, or simply smiling and being friendly. Let Stromatolite
amplify your altruistic nature. Alternatively, reach for
Stichtite, Rhodonite or Rose Quartz.

RELATIONSHIPS AND BALANCE

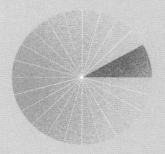

Libra season is symbolized by balanced scales.
It's a chance to look at all life areas and judge the
equilibrium. Are your relationships in balance? Do both
people in your relationships have what they want and
need? This can be a fun and harmonious time to socialize.
During Libra season, balance can also be created in your
environment through art, decoration and organization.
The scales are the symbol for justice and Libra season brings
a collective yearning to make the systems of government
more fair and to expose inequalities.

CANCER HOROSCOPE FOR LIBRA SEASON

When the Sun moves through your area
of home, family and emotions, your
natural sensitivity can become amplified.
Follow the flow of feelings. You can't
control the process, so let go and discover
where your heart takes you. Home is very
important right now – it helps to have a
cosy zone where you feel safe. Rest and
revitalize. Nurture yourself and spend
time with the people in your inner circle.

Morning Practice

Reach out and message
someone who is important to
you, and tell them why.

Evening Practice

Meditate to create
mental balance.

CRYSTALS FOR
LIBRA SEASON

HEALTHY BOUNDARIES

Iolite   Communicating what you want, need and desire is a
great starting point to gain clarity in your relationships. Iolite
can help you reflect and get to know yourself – the first step to
speaking and sharing your truth with others. Once your inner
base is stabilized, Iolite can help you reach out to another
person, while maintaining your own healthy boundaries. This
healing stone has a peaceful energy that helps you create
balance between yourself and a partner. You could also use
Amazonite, Purple Jade or Chiastolite.

BALANCE

Shungite   Balance is an active state, requiring constant
adjustment. It comes under the jurisdiction of the intellectual,
analytical sign of Libra. Keep checking in with yourself
throughout Libra season to determine what needs more
balance. For a crystal that will help you stay steady, reach for
Shungite. Or choose Diopside, Selenite or Turquoise.

DECISIVENESS

Ametrine   Libra season is an excellent time to analyse, think
things through and come up with new ideas. Keep Ametrine
by your desk for productive planning sessions and for when you
have big decisions to make. This balancing stone will help you
keep your life on track. As an alternative, try Variscite, Fluorite
or White Sapphire.

TRANSFORMATION AND FORGIVENESS

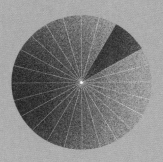

Scorpio season pulls you deeper – emotionally, physically and spiritually. This is a season of transformation, helping you to feel deeply, release old emotions and thought patterns, and get ready to move on to the next stage. By pulling back the layers and being honest with the truth of who you are, it's also an opportunity to deepen your relationships with others by letting them get to know the real you.

CANCER HOROSCOPE FOR SCORPIO SEASON

Bring out the balloons and confetti. This is your moment to party. The Sun is lighting up your area of play, fun and creativity. It's your authentic self-expression that's most important right now, so shine brightly and enjoy celebratory moments. Now is a great time to create something, even if it's jus breakfast. What matters is that you put your heart into your creativity.

Morning Practice

Forgive yourself
for something.

Evening Practice

Forgive someone else
for something.

CRYSTALS FOR
SCORPIO SEASON

INTIMACY

Red Tourmaline   Scorpio season propels you to create
warmth and closeness. But opening yourself up to the
vulnerability of intimacy demands courage. Whether you are
setting the stage for sexual intimacy or emotional intimacy,
Red Tourmaline will help you feel confident enough to
embrace deep connection with others. Other crystals for
intimacy are Garnet, Shiva Lingam or Red Aventurine.

TRANSFORMATION

Moldavite   Transformation brings both endings and
new beginnings. Moldavite will help you spiritually and
emotionally adjust when change comes into your life – when
a relationship has run its course, a shift is needed in the
work arena or a new adventure calls your name. When the
transformation you are undergoing is more subtle in texture,
like saying goodbye to an old habit, Moldavite will help you
align with your new reality. Or try Shungite, Moss Agate
or Tugtupite.

FORGIVENESS

Dioptase   Whether you need to be kinder to yourself or let go
of hurt that someone else has caused you, forgiveness doesn't
happen all at once. It's a process that you set in motion. Finding
forgiveness requires self-love, self-worth and understanding.
Dioptase can help you practice forgiveness by supporting you
with its gentle and loving vibrations. You could also turn to
Black Moonstone, Rhodochrosite or Pink Tourmaline.

WISDOM
AND FREEDOM

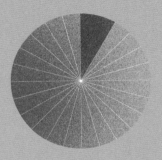

Sagittarius season is represented by the archer who shoots
high and blazes a trail into new territory. The archer is also
a centaur – half horse and half human, half wild and half
philosophical. Sagittarius season is a time to feel fiercely
alive and simultaneously inspired to ask big, existential
questions. It's a season for expanding your boundaries and
traveling physically and mentally to understand more about
the world and the human experience.

CANCER HOROSCOPE
FOR SAGITTARIUS SEASON

When you have the details sorted
out, life feels manageable, and stress
diminishes. With the Sun in your zone
of health, habits and tasks, you can get
a handle on productivity and time-
management. If these are areas where
you already excel, then take the time to
review and optimize so that your daily
life feels even easier.

Morning Practice	Evening Practice
Go for a walk or a jog out in nature.	Memorize an inspiring quote.

CRYSTALS FOR SAGITTARIUS SEASON

INNER WISDOM

Azurite   In Sagittarius season, the archer knows that the best way to take aim is to trust your inner wisdom. When you are connected to your true self, it's easier to make choices. Life feels more satisfying. Azurite is the stone to hold and carry when you want to bolster your self-confidence and tune into your wisdom. Or choose Idocrase, Shattuckite or Amethyst.

EXPANSION

Jasper   Ruled by the gas giant Jupiter, Sagittarius is the sign of expansion. During this season, you can move beyond anything that is limiting you. Is there an area of your life in which you feel trapped in a cage? Maybe if you take a closer look, you'll find that the door to the cage has been open the entire time. Feel the freedom and expansion that is available to you with the help of Jasper. This enlivening stone will help you break out into new territory. Alternatives are Blue Topaz, Pink Chalcedony or Ruby Iolite.

ADVENTURE AND TRAVEL

Turquoise   When you're setting out in search of new horizons, reach for Turquoise as your talisman for protection and luck. Travel and adventure require equal parts bravery and boldness, but the reward is an expanded mindset and perspective. Let Turquoise be your steady support system as you push beyond your boundaries to discover excitement, new opportunity and enlightenment. You could also use Green Opal, Smoky Quartz or Aventurine.

CAREER
AND GOALS

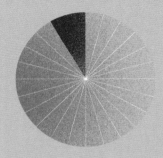

Like the mountain goat, in Capricorn season
you are primed to choose your footing carefully as
you make your ascent. Capricorn season brings practical
and productive forward motion. Use this energy efficiently
and tactically. You may choose to counterbalance this drive
and ambition with a large dose of acceptance, both
of yourself and others. Remember to give yourself a
break; you are trying your best.

CANCER HOROSCOPE
FOR CAPRICORN SEASON

The focus is on partnerships. When two people link up and a relationship is formed, there is potential for built-in support and camaraderie. There is also a lot to communicate and clarify at this time. With the Sun traversing your zone of primary partnerships, put some energy into strengthening these important bonds.

Morning Practice
Write down your goals.

Evening Practice
Reflect on your
accomplishments.

CRYSTALS FOR
CAPRICORN SEASON

ACHIEVEMENT

Fluorite   Your Capricorn season recommendation supports
you in taking things one step at a time while staying focused
on your big picture goals. Look to Fluorite. Fluorite's unique
vibration can help you concentrate, while energizing you so
that you can keep moving forwards. Or look for support from
Ocean Jasper, Septarian Nodule or Tiger's Eye.

CAREER

Cat's Eye   Capricorn season is a wonderful time to take
stock. While you think about your work life, keep Cat's Eye by
your side. This stone helps you know your strengths, which is
imperative for a fulfilling career. It will help you feel optimistic
and believe in yourself. Cat's Eye's structured energy helps
you know your personal boundaries and make smart money
choices. You could also use Andradite Garnet, Apatite or
Hawk's Eye.

FOR SELF-ACCEPTANCE

Blue Aragonite   Let calming Blue Aragonite guide you
when you need to feel the soothing balm of self-acceptance.
Capricorn season pushes you to achieve, which may cause
you to question your progress in life. Counterbalance that by
learning to accept yourself for who you are. Blue Aragonite
has a compassionate energy that may inspire you to be less
judgemental towards yourself and show yourself more kindness.
Other crystals for self-acceptance are Prasiolite, Amethyst
or Shungite.

FRIENDSHIP
AND VISION

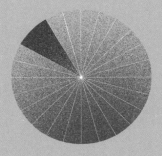

Aquarius season pushes people and ideas to the
forefront. What are your big ideas for the future?
And who is in your community? Your vision for the future
may also be a vision for humanity. Take the time to research
causes to which you might contribute time, money and
resources. Your friends, communities and social groups are
extra important during this season, so prioritize the people
who mean the most to you.

CANCER HOROSCOPE
FOR AQUARIUS SEASON

The Sun is lighting up your area of
trust and intimacy. At this time, you are
being prompted to open your heart and
love more deeply, or maybe you are in
a position to release old fears and hurts.

Think about what trust and forgiveness
means to you. These are very tricky
topics! Give these themes special
consideration and discover where you're
ready to grow.

Morning Practice

Create a vision board and make it the
first thing you see when you wake up.

Evening Practice

Call a friend for a
meaningful chat.

CRYSTALS FOR
AQUARIUS SEASON

FRIENDSHIP

Bismuth   Aquarius season asks you to turn towards your
community. What can you offer? What will you receive?
Friends enrich your life in so many ways, but mostly by
encouraging your feeling of belonging – a natural mood
booster. Bismuth has an expansive energy that helps you join
with others in a shared sense of community. Carry Bismuth as a
reminder that you are connected to others. Or you could reach
for Carnelian, Sunset Sodalite or Blue Apatite.

FAITH IN THE FUTURE

Cavansite   The future is uncertain. Sometimes you need a
boost to help you trust in the potential and possibility of what
the future can become. In that case, reach for Cavansite.
This stone has a sweet vibe of positivity that can give you the
courage to believe in your biggest dreams for the future. Some
alternatives are Peridot, Muscovite or Auralite 23.

VIBRATIONAL LIFT

Apophyllite   When Aquarius season asks you to turn
your attention to what is possible, it helps to have a positive
outlook. Without suppressing any challenging feelings (those
are important and need to be processed), pay some special
attention to the positive things in your life and work to create
an enduring, positive mindset. If you need a little extra support,
reach for Clear or Green Apophyllite. This high-vibe crystal
can lift your spirits and help you feel full of potential. You
could also try Quartz, Hematite or Angelite.

71

INTUITION AND SPIRITUALITY

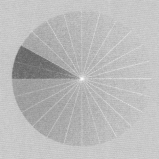

The most mystical season of all, Pisces season is the time to tune into your intuition. Slide like a slippery fish into the sphere of your dreams, faith, spirituality, compassion and creativity. This is a moment to rest, reflect and look inwards. Reconnect with your imagination. Feel your feelings. Plug into your spirituality or whatever makes you feel connected to the universe.

CANCER HOROSCOPE FOR PISCES SEASON

It's time to break old patterns by conceptualizing new beliefs and philosophies. Explore your values. What inspires you? What lights you up?

The Sun is moving through your zone of philosophy and expansion. Use this time to think big and to take action that is fuelled by your values.

Morning Practice

Record your dreams.

Evening Practice

Do some freewriting
to clear your mind.

CRYSTALS FOR
PISCES SEASON

COMPASSION

Lavender Quartz Lavender Quartz helps you feel peace and understanding for others. It will bestow upon you the softness that you need to open up to other people's perspectives. It will also allow you to dissolve drama with a heightened sense of empathy. This soothing and healing stone can offer strength while you stand in someone else's shoes. A compassionate life is a fulfilling life. As an alternative, turn to Thulite, Prehnite with Epidote or Fluorite.

INTUITION

Pink Opal When you trust your inner guidance system you have ultimate clarity. Harness the power of your intuition in Pisces season with the help of Pink Opal. This stone will help you connect to yourself and to your guides. It raises the volume on your inner 'Yes' or 'No' by quietening any distractions and helping you connect within. Other crystals for intuition are Clear Quartz, Moldavite or Dumortierite.

FOR FAITH

Celestite Faith can be thought of as a complete trust or confidence in someone or something. With a little bit of faith you may find it easier to contend with fear or anxiety. But trust and faith must be developed from within. In Pisces season, harness the power of high-vibrational Celestite to help you move beyond unnecessary fears as you put your trust in something bigger. You could also use Vatican Stone, Apophyllite or Turquoise.

LUNAR ENERGY AND MERCURY IN MOTION

THE LUNAR
CYCLE

In astrology, the Moon is a catalyst, helping us to move forwards with our goals and intentions.

The 29-day lunar cycle begins in darkness. The Moon then appears as a faint crescent and grows bigger until it's full. This process, from darkness to Full Moon, mirrors the incubation and development of your own creative process. Then, the Moon wanes until it completely disappears, reflecting another stage of the creative cycle – the process of releasing your efforts and making space for another cycle to begin. This allows new thoughts and ideas to emerge.

Each of the eight phases of the Moon cycle offers a different type of energy, which we will explore in this chapter. You can follow the Moon through the lunar month with crystal recommendations, setting your intentions in alignment with the New Moon and letting the lunar cycle help you make that intention into reality. The lunar cycle will also help you cleanse and release so that you can gently transition into the next phase.

By using crystals to work with the lunar cycle you can activate the potential of the Moon and amplify its energy. Through visualization or meditation, tap into the unique energies of each stage of the Moon cycle with the following crystals. For the suggested rituals at each phase, choose a crystal from the recommended options, or substitute with your favourite crystal.

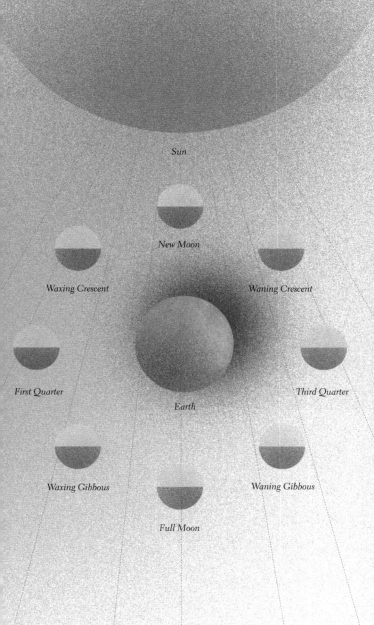

SET YOUR NEW INTENTIONS

The Moon is dark. This is a time for reflection and a time to connect with your inner self. Use your energy to envision what you would like to make happen. What do you desire? What are your dreams? Anything is possible – imagine that you are planting seeds of intention that will manifest and grow throughout the Waxing Moon Phase. The New Moon is a quiet and emotional time and you may discover that, as you think about what you would like to create, many different feelings arise. Excitement, anticipation, fear, worry – whatever feelings arise, make space for those feelings and be gentle with yourself. Listen to your intuition and imagine your next steps.

Black Moonstone can support you during the delicate and sensitive New Moon vibration. It offers wellsprings of patience and peace as you work with your emotions and reflect on your life. When your dreams are germinating under the surface, Black Moonstone can help you trust your own process.

Labradorite opens your third eye wide so that you can tune into your intuition and design your goals in accordance with your path and purpose.

Pink Sapphire's loving energy can buffer you and help you feel emotionally at ease.

Ametrine provides sweet joy and concentrated focus so that you can set intentions with confidence.

TRUST,
INSPIRATION, SERENITY
AND DELIGHT

New Moon Ritual

Freewrite about what you yearn for and anything else that's on your mind. Then jot down your intentions for this Moon cycle on a piece of paper and place your chosen crystal on top.

NURTURE YOUR INTENTIONS

Your seeds of intention are germinating under the soil, and maybe some of the plants are just beginning to sprout. As the lunar energy builds momentum, make sure that you have the resources you need to achieve your goals. Provide structure and support for yourself. This cycle is just beginning to take shape, so consider how your choices will determine your direction – maybe there are changes you'd like to make to your goals. Remain curious throughout this process, because anything is possible!

Turquoise is a powerhouse of a crystal that can deftly carry you through the precarious Waxing Crescent phase. At this moment you need a subtle combination of confidence, discernment, curiosity and commitment. Turquoise can help you understand the truth of what you need to create, and it can help you stay open and accepting of your process. Use this stone as you decide what you really want to manifest and commit to during this Moon cycle.

Shattuckite helps you intuitively illuminate your path so that you can make the decisions that are right for you.

Pyrite offers crystalline protection and is a wonderful choice to help you realize your goals.

Orange Calcite gives you mental focus and lots of energy for the journey ahead.

TRUTH,
INTUITION, MANIFESTATION
AND FOCUS

Waxing Crescent Moon Ritual

Read and rewrite your intentions for this Moon cycle.
Decorate the paper and place your chosen crystal back on top.

BUILD YOUR MOMENTUM

Look around your garden of intentions and discover what is growing. Have your goals started to take shape? If so, how are they coming along? Do you need more support? Perhaps you have had surprising results? At the First Quarter Moon the constraints of reality can be intimidating. You have big dreams, but sometimes you encounter resistance when dreams make contact with real world limitations. Maybe there is more work required than you had foreseen, or there are real-world issues with time, money, support or other resources. Give yourself lots of encouragement. Pivot, and reassess if necessary. This is an exciting, high energy time, so keep taking action and building momentum.

Bumblebee Jasper When reality, and all of its limitations, hits, Bumblebee Jasper can help you stay the course with confidence. Lean on this crystal when you need the energy to just keep moving forwards. It will subdue your fears and inspire you to push past your comfort zone.

Peridot is a cheery companion that will help you look at any situation with optimism.

Tangerine Quartz offers creative potential that makes problem solving effortless.

Aventurine will vitalize you and give you the confidence to keep going.

CONFIDENCE,
OPTIMISM, CREATIVITY AND
VITALITY

First Quarter Moon Ritual

Light a candle, hold your chosen crystal and visualize your intentions being realized.

DEVELOP YOUR INTENTIONS

It's astonishing what a little effort can create! Now that you've made it to the Waxing Gibbous phase of the Moon cycle, you are starting to see the effects of the intentions that you set. If your goal was to improve your nutrition, you may be feeling better already. If you felt motivated to get out there and start dating, you may have started some new conversations. Whatever the last few days have revealed, now is the time to roll up your sleeves and actively give shape to your garden. What will you weed out? What is working, and what isn't working? What changes might you make? The intensity has almost peaked to take tender care of your emotional well-being as you keep putting in effort towards your dreams.

Jet Jet's grounding energy will help you establish deep root systems for your developing intentions. When you need strength and motivation to keep pushing forwards with your goals, this stone will support you. As a bonus, jet has a sheltering vibration that can steady you emotionally and help you surge forwards with optimism and hope.

Hematite offers balance and protection, helping you proactively take care of yourself during this active time.

Carnelian lights your fire with sparkling enthusiasm and convinces you to tune into your creative side.

Blue Lace Agate calms your mind, allowing you to weed through your options and make solid decisions.

GROUNDING,
PROTECTION, ENTHUSIASM
AND PEACE OF MIND

Waxing Gibbous Moon Ritual

While holding or wearing your chosen crystal, do something that feels active or expressive, such as dancing, painting, gardening, cooking or singing. Imagine your goals and repeat your intentions.

HARVEST

Everything is revealed under the light of the Moon. The attempts you've made, your wins, your losses. It's time to get out in the garden and harvest the crop. Regardless of whether the bounty lives up to your expectations, there is something to appreciate and celebrate. At the Full Moon, honour what you've created and give gratitude to yourself for your commitment. This phase represents the push and pull of two opposite energies as the Moon is in the opposite sign to the Sun. The result is a highly polarized and intense energy that can heighten emotions, pull you in two different directions, or cause you to realize something important. Make sure to be very gentle with yourself and those around you.

White Moonstone symbolizes the Full Moon and all of its glorious creativity and excitement. This pearly white crystal shines a bright light so that you can see clearly. As you examine the fruits that you've cultivated during the Waxing Moon phase, use the receptive and healing energy of White Moonstone to help you accept and celebrate. It's time for gratitude, and this comforting crystal will help you open up to that feeling.

Green Apatite is an antidote to the drama of the Full Moon – use it to highlight joy and abundance.

Jade has a subtle, soothing energy that imparts an optimistic attitude.

Stilbite connects the heart, mind and intuition – this can help you rationally balance your emotions while still opening up to divine insight.

EMOTIONAL EXPLORATION, ABUNDANCE, PEACEFULNESS AND RECEPTIVITY

Full Moon Ritual

Hold your chosen crystal and write down three things that you are grateful for. The Full Moon is also a great time to cleanse your crystals. Place them outside or on a windowsill and let them bathe in the Moon's healing energy.

Now that the intensity of the full reveal has begun to wane, you can settle deeper into your new reality. Indulge yourself and enjoy. As the Moon has moved through waxing to waning, this is the beginning of a less active and more receptive phase. This means that you can simply sit with the ebbing fullness of what is. Begin a process of compassionate review. What have you learned? What will you do differently in the next Moon cycle? Each lunar cycle reveals an older, more experienced version of who you are becoming. So sink into this moment of reflection and get to know yourself once more.

Obsidian offers a protective energy that buffers and supports. Use it at the Waning Gibbous phase of the Moon cycle to release the past and securely recline into the experience of the moment. Obsidian's cleansing vibes can help you remove any junk from your thought patterns, allowing you to think from a new perspective. Harness its clarifying energy to appraise your situation with equanimity and objectivity.

Tiger's Eye is for encouragement and strength as you review your progress and make plans for improvement.

Citrine offers joy and optimism so that you can look at your accomplishments through a positive lens.

Celestite provides tranquillity as you come down off the high of the Full Moon.

PROTECTION, STRENGTH, JOY AND TRANQUILLITY

Waning Gibbous Moon Ritual

Pour yourself some tea, water, or other drink of your choice, and take the time to sit and quietly appreciate the moment. With your chosen crystal nearby, review your intention and gratitude lists.

LET GO

Get comfortable letting go so that you can make space for new things. At the Last Quarter Moon allow the leaves to fall and the fading plants to return to the soil. A tree drops its leaves to conserve resources. Take stock of what you want to let go of, so that you can use your energy wisely. Is there someone you need to forgive? Do you need to release your expectations and accept something about your life? Release the past or an outdated way of thinking, let go and forgive. Maybe you declutter your closet, acknowledge your reality, admit your mistakes, get really honest with yourself, or forgive yourself or others. The Last Quarter Moon asks that you put in a little effort to let go of the emotions and ideas that are taking up excess energy.

LOVE, SUPPORT, GROUNDING AND GENTLE SELF-REFLECTION

Rose Quartz is an emotional balm that can help you forgive yourself and others. As the Last Quarter Moon inspires you to release your expectations and accept your current reality, you need a soothing support that helps you open up compassionately. Rose Quartz brings playful, loving vibes and helps you gently accept a situation and move forwards.

Rutilated Quartz offers a powerful support in following through on your intentions as you review what you've learned and plan for the next phase.

Smoky Quartz provides grounding, protection and assistance in clearing the thoughts and feelings that you are ready to release.

Amethyst is for gently releasing old mental patterns and contemplating new possibilities.

Last Quarter Moon Ritual

Create a peaceful environment and run a bath for yourself. Place a water-safe, non-toxic crystal (such as Quartz or Amethyst) in the bath while you review your intentions from this moon cycle. Repeat these affirmations, 'I make space for clarity' and 'I release the past'.

STILLNESS AND REST

The lunar energy is encouraging you to turn inwards and be still. All is quiet in the winter of your metaphorical garden. Embracing stillness offers many benefits. By allowing your inner landscape to exist without judgement, you honour who you are now. Slowing down can also help you uncover your values and emotional truth – which may not be so apparent when you are busily running around. And last but not least, rest and quiet will help you recharge your energy for the next cycle. Challenge yourself to slow down and be present in the moment. There will be ample time for new plans and dreams when the next cycle begins.

Serpentine can help you open a gateway to the stillness within and to the profound interconnectedness of the universe. Using this crystal during your Waning Crescent Moon meditations will help you feel buffered and supported in the understanding that there is no-one you need to be and nothing you need to do. Float along with the waves of existence. You'll know when the time is right again for action.

Selenite radiates cleansing energy that can help you release the past cycle and prepare to make a fresh start.

Howlite soothes your spirit and quietens any absurd complaints from your 'inner critic'.

Aquamarine helps you create a meditative state of mind so that you can listen to the stillness within.

CONNECTION WITH NATURE, CLEANSING, SOOTHING AND REFLECTION

Waning Crescent Moon Ritual

Sit quietly in the meditation of your choosing. Hold your crystal or place it nearby.

MERCURY
RETROGRADE

Mercury Retrograde deserves attention as it's a chance to review your plans and goals. It's notoriously known for causing technology and communication issues, but the upside of this time period is that it offers an invitation to slow down and re-assess where you are and where you want to go.

Fast-moving Mercury symbolizes connection, communication and technology. Mercury is the part of you that learns, thinks, teaches and talks.

Mercury orbits the Sun about four times as fast as the Earth and every time that Mercury zips past the Earth an optical illusion occurs that makes it look as though Mercury is moving backwards. When Mercury appears to be moving backwards (Mercury Retrograde), it's a great opportunity to slow down. Go back over your thoughts and decisions of recent months and review them. Turn inwards to gain guidance from your intuition.

Mercury Retrograde happens about three times a year and lasts for about three weeks each time. You can use these retrograde periods as a moment to check in with yourself and review your practices, thoughts and relationships. Have you been putting off an uncomfortable conversation? Is there something that you need to be honest about with yourself when it comes to relationships, work or money? What has your body been trying to tell you? Is there some new way that you could step out of your comfort zone? What would help you feel more secure and supported?

Underlying issues tend to rise to the surface during Mercury Retrograde. It's typically advised to make sure that you are extra clear in your communications during these periods, and that you wait until the retrograde period has ended before beginning new projects or signing contracts. But it's an excellent time to pick up where you left off on something – to rethink, redo and review.

YOUR CRYSTAL PRACTICE DURING MERCURY RETROGRADE

Crystal energy can help you slow down your busy mind and tune into your intuition during Mercury Retrograde. As you rethink and review, these crystals will amplify your intuition and clarity.

KEEN INSIGHT

Pietersite Employ this speckled Quartz for illuminated insight paired with steady determination.

CLARITY AND COMMUNICATION

Aquamarine This stone soothes and calms the mind while simultaneously boosting your ability to communicate clearly.

CREATIVE THOUGHT

Citrine A crystal that spurs your imagination, helping you conceptualize how you might like patterns or situations to change.

Beginning of Mercury Retrograde Ritual

Perform a full and gentle review of the issues most affecting you by writing a journal entry using the following prompt: 'What do I need to see that I'm not seeing when it comes to my …' Give yourself lots of gratitude in the process and call on your chosen crystal to provide understanding and clarity. When you've finished, write down three takeaways on a small piece of paper and place your crystal on top of it for the remainder of the Retrograde. Drawing on the power of your crystal, let your subconscious mind continue to explore and reveal the subtleties of these thoughts and questions over the coming weeks.

End of Mercury Retrograde Ritual

Near the end of the Retrograde cycle, set an intention to integrate what you've learned during the past days and weeks. Begin by returning to your piece of paper and your crystal. What came up for you during Mercury Retrograde? Was there a new realization, attitude or interest that emerged? Think about what you may have realized and journal about what you'd like to bring into your life now. Is there an intention (see page 22) or affirmation that could come from this exploration? If so, write it down. Look in a mirror and repeat your intention or affirmation five times while holding your crystal. Remember to thank your crystal and to thank yourself for showing up. For the next two weeks, repeat this daily ritual.

CONCLUSION

This book has taken you deep below the Earth's surface, through the metaphorical caverns of crystals and their symbolism. You've connected the dots of the solar system and the meaning of the astrology you were born with. By pairing the forces of the stars above with the crystals below, you've gained tools that can help you navigate your unique journey with wisdom.

In Part Two, you learned about the crystals that can support your unique astrology. This section included insights for Cancer Sun, Moon and Rising signs, along with supportive crystal recommendations for what your sign needs in five key life areas.

Life is always changing and so in Part Three you learned to follow the energy of the Sun as it moves on its annual journey through the zodiac, finding crystals that may help you elaborate on the theme of each astrological season.

Revolving and evolving with changing astrological cycles continued in Part Four, where you paired crystal energy with the ebb and flow of the Moon, and learned to harness the power of crystals in tandem with Mercury Retrograde to perform a trimonthly check-in.

All the answers are already within you. When you choose a crystal, you awaken the vibration of that crystal within yourself. Harness your astro-crystal practice to help you see what already exists inside of you. You have everything you need.

With the cosmos above and the crystals below, you are always connected and supported. Let the stones and the stars strengthen your self-awareness and self-trust as you continue your crystalline cosmic journey.

Crystals and astrology are not intended to be a substitute for medical advice, diagnosis or treatment. Always seek the advice of your qualified healthcare provider.

RESOURCES

GET YOUR BIRTH CHART

www.sandysitron.com/crystals

ASTROLOGY READING

www.sandysitron.com

CRYSTALS

101 Power Crystals: *The Ultimate Guide to Magical Crystals, Gems, and Stones for Healing and Transformation*
Judy Hall

CRYSTAL ENERGY HEALING

https://www.kalisaaugustine.com/

SOURCING CRYSTALS RESPONSIBLY

moonrisecrystals.com/

SPIRAL CRYSTALS

spiralcrystals.com/

HOOF AND PAW

hoofandpawuk.com/

ASTROLOGY

Astrology for Yourself
Demetra George and Douglas Bloch

AFFIRMATION WORK

Transformational coach Dana Balicki:
https://danabalicki.com/

AFFIRMATION WORK

Empowerment: *The Art of Creating Your Life as You Want It*
Gail Straub and David Gershon

ASTROLOGY EDUCATION

www.thestrology.com

Ritual Enchantments
A Modern Witch's Guide to Self-Possession
Mya Spalter

FEATURED CRYSTALS

First published in Great Britain in 2022 by Laurence King
an imprint of The Orion Publishing Group Ltd
Carmelite House, 50 Victoria Embankment
London EC4Y 0DZ

An Hachette UK Company

10 9 8 7 6 5 4 3 2 1

A CIP catalogue record for this book is
available from the British Library.

ISBN 978-0-8578-2924-5

Design: Therese Vandling

Printed in China by C&C Offset Printing Co. Ltd

Laurence King Publishing is committed to ethical and
sustainable production. We are proud participants in the
Book Chain Project®. [bookchainproject.com]

www.laurenceking.com
www.orionbooks.co.uk